FLOOR ABOVE THE ROOF
(a drama in one act)

by

Daniel Therriault

BROADWAY PLAY PUBLISHING INC
New York
www.broadwayplaypublishing.com
info@broadwayplaypublishing.com

FLOOR ABOVE THE ROOF

Copyright 1984 by Daniel Therriault

All rights reserved. This work is fully protected under the copyright laws of the United States of America.

No part of this publication may be photocopied, reproduced, stored in a retrieval system, or transmitted, in any form or by any means, electronic, mechanical, recording, or otherwise without the prior permission of the publisher. Additional copies of this play are available from the publisher.

Written permission is required for live performance of any sort. This includes readings, cuttings, scenes, and excerpts. For amateur and stock performance, please contact Broadway Play Publishing, Inc.

For all other rights, please contact Leah Schmidt, c/o Rosenstone-Wender, 3 East 48 Street, New York, NY 10017.

First printing: April 1984

ISBN: 0-88145-015-4

Design by Marie Donovan
Set in Baskerville by L&F Technical Composition, Lakeland, FL

To

Nikos, Laurie, and Melanie

CHARACTERS

Elroy	Black male
Cantor	Black male
Jay	Black male
Swifty	White male

The entire action takes place in the freight elevator lobby of a warehouse on Twentieth Street and Broadway in New York City.

The time is the present.

All action occurs within the period of one August working day.

SYNOPSIS OF SCENES
Scene One: Morning
Scene Two: Afternoon

Scene One

The elevator lobby area is small and claustrophobic. Against one wall, a radiator with a board laid across the top is used as a two-seater bench. There are a few garbage cans laden with trash, as well as plastic bags filled with junk. The centerpiece of the room is a large, steel-door elevator. When slammed shut, the door clangs with the finality of a cell. An imaginary street runs across the apron of the stage providing entranceways from both left and right. There is also an entrance from a stairwell upstage. The air hangs hazy and oppressive on an already muggy morning in mid-August. ELROY *enters from the street. He sips coffee through a hole punched into the plastic cover of a paper cup, and eats a donut. He wears a dark blue work uniform. He goes to the elevator and unlocks the door with a load of keys that he wears on a pullstring attached to his belt. The elevator is manually operated, so he carries a rag for the friction. Suddenly he double-takes, and his eyes arrest upon a point behind a garbage can.*

ELROY: What you doing my man? And I ain't rapping to the can. (*A voice from behind the garbage can answers.*)

VOICE: Thought I'd get to work early.

ELROY: You ain't never been before nine-thirty.

VOICE: Don't tell what I already know.

ELROY: Where're your eyes? I'm looking at two drops of blood. Like your nose is parting the Red Sea.

VOICE: I ain't used to getting up this early.

ELROY: More like staying up this late. (*The* VOICE *laughs.*) How come you laying there like a sack of garbage?

VOICE: Who you calling what?

ELROY: I call them like I see them; and you struck out. (*The* VOICE *rumbles a low laugh.*)

VOICE: Well, ump, you got something for the head?

ELROY: I know you don't mean aspirin.

VOICE: Straight.

ELROY: All I got is a hit of chocolate speed. Take this. (*He offers his coffee.*) I'm not sinking down to your level. Climb up to mine.

(*The* VOICE *moans. A hand raises and grips the top of the can.* CANTOR *struggles to his feet. He wears a large-brimmed hat with a feather at a rakish angle. He dresses in purple and green clothes like the plumage of a peacock, and wears shiny shoes and nylon stockings. As he reaches for the coffee, his other hand drifts into his back pocket and pulls out a pint of Wild Turkey whiskey. He pours a bit into the coffee.*)

CANTOR: Elroy, I need a hair of the mutt.

ELROY: Cantor, you need a pelt of the pack. (CANTOR *laughs and takes a large gulp of the drink.*) Lucky you didn't sit down hard, you'd of cut your backside.

CANTOR: (*Laughing.*) This Cantor may be singing—

ELROY: You hitting a high note.

CANTOR: — but I don't spill the Fountain of Youth. (*He slugs hard at the drink.*)

ELROY: Youth? I'm looking in the face of a dead man.

SCENE ONE

CANTOR: We all dead, man. The liability of birth is death. The only thing you're responsible for. The privilege to be born is the same privilege to die. The one thing you can depend on. All us folks living going to be dying. I'm just going out with a bang.

ELROY: Think you need another hit.

CANTOR: I maintain the right to kill myself by the way I live. I don't give no one else that pleasure. I'll die by life. Not be dead while I'm living.

ELROY: I've seen some cadavers look better than you. (*Pause.*) Personally I don't start exercising my elbow 'til noon. But I guess you don't stop drinking 'til then.

CANTOR: Why put pleasure on a time schedule? Strap a muzzle on your fun, and you'll never take a full bite out of life.

ELROY: You're the preacher.

CANTOR: Straight.

ELROY: But you ain't never been like this. This ain't you. And you ain't having fun. So don't pull the wool. The heat's on, no snowjobs. Serious, sucker, what's on your mind?

(*The air blasts with hot, sexy, disco-funk dance music. The music gets louder as* JAY *and* SWIFTY *get closer.* CANTOR *slips on a pair of sunglasses and pockets his bottle.* JAY *enters with a definite suave step. He has a huge box radio strapped on his shoulder and a lit joint clenched between his teeth as he sashays into the lobby. He speaks with a Trinidad accent.* SWIFTY *follows him up, also moving to the music. He dances and balances a cup of coffee without spilling a drop. They both wear heavy work boots, tee shirts, and dungarees. When they enter,* CANTOR *backs into a wall with his hands covering his ears.*)

CANTOR: (*Yelling.*) Cut the funk, punk!

JAY: Free country.

CANTOR: And I'm free to plant my fist down your throat!

JAY: You don't like my music?

CANTOR: Much as you like to eat knuckles.

JAY: You had — how you say — a "bad night"?

CANTOR: Shut the box!

JAY: You not asking nice?

CANTOR: You asking for a nice broke face!

JAY: Okay, man. I take pity on the poor of spirit. (*He smiles and turns off the radio.*)

SWIFTY: (*He stops dancing.*) Hey what's cooking? That juice is my ham and eggs.

JAY: (*With mock concern.*) Tsk, tsk, tsk. Have you no heart, Swifty? Can you not see the man is in pain?

CANTOR: I'm getting a cup of coffee.

ELROY: As a mixer?

JAY: I don't need Maxwell House to get me perking. A woman wakes up a man better than any coffee bean. And this morning I had my woman black, a lot of sugar, with cream.

(JAY *blasts the radio loudly.* SWIFTY *and* JAY *laugh and dance.* ELROY *smiles.* JAY *turns off the radio.* CANTOR *begins to exit, then stops and turns.*)

CANTOR: (*To* JAY.) Hey, before I blow, though, where's my AM/FM?

JAY: What say, man?

CANTOR: I saw you unloading some frozen music boxes last night, and I'd say those radios are still on ice. Very cool without recorded numbers.

JAY: You do like ice cream, don't you.

CANTOR: Got a sweet tooth for whatever's free.

JAY: What you got for me on the rocks?

CANTOR: What you want?

JAY: Your girlfriend's telephone number. (*He blasts the radio on, laughs, and then turns it off.*)

CANTOR: Immigrant. I'm to the store. (*He turns to leave.*)

JAY: Hey, Cant, just kidding, man. I respect family. I miss my mother in Trinidad. (*Seriously.*) Your mother is still alive, right?

CANTOR: Yeah.

JAY: Then give me her phone number! (*He blasts on the radio, dances and laughs.*)

CANTOR: You want your nose on the left side of your face?

JAY: (*He turns off the radio.*) You got threads up there, right?

CANTOR: You know what I got. The latest fashions in designer clothes. The best labels in shirts, suits, and jackets.

JAY: But Italian.

SWIFTY: Dago delight.

CANTOR: They ain't bad. In fact, I just got in a load. Lightweight and slick. There was a box of fifty-one jackets when supposed to be only half a hundred.

JAY: What color?

CANTOR: Turquoise. (JAY *makes a disgusted noise.*) What's wrong with that? I dig turquoise.

JAY: I would, too, if I was a peacock.

SWIFTY: Turquoise has got an edge. I'll take one.

CANTOR: You take nothing. I only got one, and it's expensive.

SWIFTY: I can get you a radio that's a Hawaiian girl in a grass skirt. The tuner and volume controls are her knobs.

CANTOR: No junk, punk. I want a serious radio, not that novelty type. All your boss got up there is toys.

SWIFTY: Your clothes upstairs is foreign and out of fashion. No class act wants to wear that iridescent look.

CANTOR: (*Sharply to* SWIFTY) This jacket goes for ninety-five dollars wholesale, jack, and you trying to jack me around with jacks and jumpropes, jackass! How about it, Jay-man? Clean piece of cloth.

JAY: I don't like turquoise.

(CANTOR *sees a woman approaching. Whenever a woman passes, though she is not visible, the men watch her walk on the street, passing from stage right to left and vice-versa.*)

Scene One

CANTOR: Oh my lord.

SWIFTY: Here we go.

JAY: (*To the woman.*) You should be arrested. Serving time for second-degree murder, 'cause you're killing me, lady. Help, police! You're stabbing me with those eyes. You criminal.

SWIFTY: You know you're helping break up a marriage when you wear those red shorts? Think of my kids, you shameless wonder. Nylons with spike heels.

CANTOR: You getting me bigger than I already am. I'll do you a favor, baby, got some knee pads in the back. (*She is gone.*)

SWIFTY: You're crude, man.

CANTOR: And you're honkey.

SWIFTY: And you're a dumb nigger.

CANTOR: What you say, pale?

JAY: He said you're a dumb nigger, and you are, so shut up.

CANTOR: Say hey, albino, leave the black beauties to us.

SWIFTY: Then you put a clamp on your lips the next time a polished piece of ivory comes slipping down the street, check? (*They all laugh.*)

CANTOR: Wicked. You're right, white, they're all ours. Every joker for himself.

JAY: (*To* SWIFTY) I'll take a novelty radio off your hands.

SWIFTY: I don't need no box radio.

JAY: You want the jacket, right?

SWIFTY: I said so.

JAY: Then give me a toy radio a little girl would like.

SWIFTY: I don't need nothing you got.

CANTOR: I need the vibe machine.

SWIFTY: I want the turquoise.

JAY: And I have to have toys.

CANTOR: What you want with a bunch of trinkets?

SWIFTY: You ain't got no kids.

CANTOR: Ain't into child molesting, are you?

SWIFTY: Ain't none of your family here.

JAY: You want to light up the night with those glow-in-the-dark lapels?

SWIFTY: Be looking boss.

JAY: (*To* CANTOR.) You want the battery box?

CANTOR: Ain't that what I been saying?

JAY: (*To* CANTOR.) You give Swifty the jacket. I give you the radio. Swifty, you give me a Santa's bag full of toys. (CANTOR *and* SWIFTY *exchange looks.*) A deal?

CANTOR: Straight.

Scene One

SWIFTY: Even.

JAY: Balanced.

(*They see some women approaching.* JAY *breaks into a mock-sentimental, soul-type, love song.* CANTOR *and* SWIFTY *join in immediately, as this is one of their routines. They sing back-up harmony during the chorus and "ooh-aah" vocals during the spoken verse. They step in choreographed movements and extend pleading gestures toward the women who pass by during the song.*)

JAY, CANTOR, and SWIFTY:

CHORUS: My crippled heart hangs / limp in your hand
I love you more / in one glance / than any man can

Spoken (JAY): Oh mamma, you hurting my heart
You move me, in my every body part

Oh darling, don't do me wrong
After you made me, get this long

CHORUS: My crippled heart hangs / limp in your hand
I love you more / in one glance / than any man can

(*The women are gone.*)

JAY: We're settled, then.

SWIFTY: Placid.

CANTOR: Serene.

SWIFTY: My wife says I look sexy in turquoise.

CANTOR: Laverne has always wanted a box radio. Now she got one.

SWIFTY: And a pair of sunglasses, Cantor. Cool blue tints. I'll be looking iced.

CANTOR: You got it. Laverne'll think it's her birthday. She'll give me a big hug.

SWIFTY: I'll be looking so cool, my wife'll get hot.

JAY: (*To* SWIFTY.) I need a child's doll. They make black ones here?

SWIFTY: Got 'em.

JAY: Make it pretty.

SWIFTY: I'll get one that wets.

CANTOR: She'll be crazy for me.

SWIFTY: (*To* CANTOR.) Class glass. Not like that piece of plastic you got strapped around your temples to hold your brain in.

CANTOR: You can wrap your thin lips around my you-know.

SWIFTY: I got to shove. I don't get up there, Boneface is going to kick, and you know who.

JAY: Later, Swift.

CANTOR: See ya.

(SWIFTY *crosses to the elevator.*)

ELROY: Say, Cant. Could you get me a pair of shades, too?

Scene One

CANTOR: Sure thing.

ELROY: The kind that wrap around the corner of your eye. You can look sideways and no one knows.

CANTOR: Straight.

(SWIFTY *and* ELROY *go up in the elevator as* JAY *sees another woman.*)

JAY: Oh momma, oh daddy, oh little sister. Check the chick with the—

JAY *and* CANTOR: (*Simultaneously.*) Ice cream cone! (*They both moan.*)

CANTOR: (*To the woman.*) Me and you are blue, baby. You're a blue movie and I'm blue balls.

JAY: (*To* CANTOR.) Catch the tongue, man.

CANTOR: (*To the woman.*) You can't walk down this street like that.

JAY: (*To the woman, very sweetly.*) Can I have some? Can I have some? Pretty please.

CANTOR: You move your hips like that, you got to wiggle down another street!

JAY: Just a little? One tiny lick?

CANTOR: I said don't shake those hips sideways. You hear? You hypnotizing me. I said stop that hip action, you cruel thing! (*She is gone.*)

JAY: What you check a chick with first?

CANTOR: She be walking down the street?

JAY: And looking very good, man.

CANTOR: She throwing that sweet funk in my face? First I catch her lips. They juicy, I go slam down to her belly. She pass by—bam—I hit her in the rear. But sometimes I go (*He looks left.*) breast (*He looks straight.*), loin (*He looks right.*), rump.

JAY: Sounds like a butcher shop. I peer into her eyes. Do that mind control to get her to look at me. Then I don't mess around. I go for the throat. The most vulnerable area. When a woman puts her head back and shows you her throat, she's open to you. Then I drop to her feet in veneration. Top to bottom in one glance. I suss her whole being. Then I shinny slowly up her legs. I love grasshopper legs. I climb miles of thighs to get to where it counts.

(SWIFTY *and* ELROY *emerge from the elevator.* SWIFTY *pushes a handtruck strapped with a couple of boxes. The next section builds in rhythm and intensity. The dialogue can overlap.*)

CANTOR: I like thighs in the shower. I drop the soap a lot.

JAY: Her tiny toes turn white gripping the porcelain.

CANTOR: My girlfriend's a vampire. She devours everything in sight. She lying on her side, I look bottom, top, lips.

SWIFTY: My wife's in the sack. I rip off the sheet and go thighs, belly, eyes.

JAY: The little place behind her ears.

CANTOR: Nose, cheeks, forehead.

Scene One

SWIFTY: Inside of her elbows.

CANTOR: Her tongue.

JAY: Soft spot under her tongue.

CANTOR: Teeth.

SWIFTY: Kiss her temples.

JAY: Get lost in her hair.

CANTOR: Back of her knees.

JAY: Nape of the neck.

SWIFTY: Arches of her feet.

CANTOR: Small of her back.

JAY: Skin under her chin.

SWIFTY: Inside her mouth.

JAY: Grip her hips.

CANTOR: Grab and jab.

(*The following three lines are said simultaneously.*)

CANTOR: I call head and tail, I never lose.

SWIFTY: Flip her over. Backside best.

JAY: Any way she wants. I can tell the way she moves.

SWIFTY: She don't make a sound but her eyes are fire.

JAY: Whimpers in little cries.

CANTOR: Always lets loose. Screaming like a banshee!

SWIFTY: She smiles and watches me. Flushed all red.

JAY: Her face twisted in pain. Tears run down her cheeks.

CANTOR: The noises that bust out of her!

SWIFTY: Her mouth opens but not a whisper. Not a sigh.

JAY: She sobs. I wipe her face.

CANTOR: She don't know where she's at. Like she's crazy!

SWIFTY: Soft.

CANTOR: Hard.

JAY: Sad.

SWIFTY: Silent.

CANTOR: Loud.

JAY: She cries.

(*The three men fall silent, each lost in the image of his woman. They look at each other and laugh. Then they speak quickly.*)

JAY: She's sensually supra-sensational.

CANTOR: Laverne do anything for her man!

SWIFTY: I can't imagine more than my wife. (*Pause.*)

Scene One

ELROY: Snap out of it, hornies. Y'all late but Swifty.

JAY: Man-oh-man!

ELROY: (*Going to* SWIFTY) You got time to pick me up some coffee on the way back, Swift?

SWIFTY: Sure, El. Black.

ELROY: (*Nodding and giving him coins.*) Top floor. (*To* CANTOR.) You planning on getting fired today?

CANTOR: I'm getting my own coffee.

ELROY: Take care of yourself. (ELROY *and* JAY *go up in the elevator.*)

CANTOR: Say, Elevator-man never say nothing to blackberry pies on the street or joins in when we're talking to get a bulge.

SWIFTY: I hear what you're saying and I know.

CANTOR: Yet he gets more of that sweet stuff than any of us.

SWIFTY: He's got them running on a schedule.

CANTOR: Takes them down to his basement penthouse.

SWIFTY: You ever been to his pad downstairs?

CANTOR: I got my beak in once. Looked like a lot of leopard skin.

SWIFTY: How's he do it?

CANTOR: What do chicks see in him?

SWIFTY: How's he come on to them?

CANTOR: He's got four kids and a beautiful wife at home.

(ELROY *comes out of the shaft.* SWIFTY *begins to leave with his handtruck.*)

SWIFTY: Black.

ELROY: Top floor.

(SWIFTY *exists.* CANTOR *takes off his sunglasses and finishes off the bottle of whiskey. His one knee buckles. The two men stare at each other for a moment.*)

ELROY: You're trying to flush something out of your system.

CANTOR: Later.

ELROY: More Wild Turkey for a dead peacock?

CANTOR: I can still spread my tail. (*He struts away.*)

ELROY: Better keep your beak clean. In jail, you be spreading tail more than you want.

BLACKOUT

[END OF SCENE ONE]

SCENE TWO

Afternoon. JAY *pours rum into a cola bottle.* CANTOR *sips Wild Turkey, and* ELROY *drinks a beer.* JAY *and* CANTOR *pass a joint.* ELROY *does not indulge. The air, humid and unhealthy, boils at the stifling peak of the August day.*

CANTOR: You could slice the air with a switchblade and pan-fry an enchilada on this lobby floor.

JAY: Can't even see across the river, so hazy.

CANTOR: (*Screaming.*) I'm hot!

JAY: The stink of garbage so bad my lunch tasted like coffee grinds, empty milk cartons, and egg shells.

CANTOR: Cigar butts, rotten catfish, and bad limburger.

JAY: Want to make me puke.

CANTOR: Pollution poking me in the eyes. They're burning red.

JAY (*Indicating the joint.*) That's from the Ganje, man.

ELROY: That liquor don't help neither.

CANTOR: The booze-blood boiling in my veins is life, my man! My life! The life I'm living! I answer to no one. This city got me beat. (*Holding up the bottle.*) I need this fire (*Gesturing outward to the street.*) to break this fever! (*He takes a hit from the bottle.*)

JAY: It's never this hot in my country.

CANTOR: You're crazy! Trinidad's closer to the equator. That island must be like an oil slick ablaze in the middle of the ocean.

JAY: Manhattan is the jungle island with the heat wave, man. In Trinidad, the Caribbean breezes touch your body like soft, cool fingers. You come out of the light blue water across cool white sand, raise your arms, and small gusts blow on you like the fresh breath of a young girl. It tingles. Perfection. Paradise. Here, you never get that feeling of being both warm and cool. Only freezing or boiling.

CANTOR: Yeah? If it's so cool, why ain't you back there having them wind women licking you all over the place?

JAY: (*He laughs.*) The fruit trees, the birds, the sea are all paradise. But there's no Utopia when you're hungry, man.

CANTOR: (*Hotheadedly.*) I busted loose of Harlem, but I'm still hungry! You think you're getting anywhere with work like this? This job is a swift kick in the groin. (*Sarcastically angry.*) Since you're a virgin in this country, somebody better bust your cherry. Get you hip to the facts of life. The birds and the bees in these United States runs like this: YOU GET SCREWED. Short and simple. There's no way out. I ain't got nowhere and there ain't nowhere to go. It ain't me. And it ain't you. We're at the mercy of the structure. Always was. Is now. And always will be. Amen. That's the Bible of this country. (*With emphasis.*) If this country was a building, we'd be in a busted elevator, stuck between two lower floors, and nobody is calling the repairman. (*He takes a massive swallow of liquor.*)

JAY: I escaped my country. I made it happen. Me. Alone. Me. This job saved me.

CANTOR: A job pushing junk around from one rich man to another. I don't care where you been or where you're going, but for right now, we ain't only in the same boat, the same country, the same culture, same island bordered on the same ocean, we ain't only on the same street, we're in the same damn shaft! We're all the same. (*Pointing.*) Me, you, and you! And there's nothing we can do about it. Resign yourself to the facts.

JAY: (*Defiantly.*) I don't resign myself to nothing.

CANTOR: You're floating in the same toilet as us.

ELROY: (*To* CANTOR.) Curb it, man. Put a pooper scooper under your chin.

CANTOR: Say what you say?

ELROY: Just trying to clean up the conversation. (*Pause. Simply.*) I like this job. If I didn't have this job, I don't know what else I'd do. It's a good job. I like this job. It's a good job.

(*The elevator bell rings.*)

JAY: That's my man, El. Where else can you get high and paid for it? (JAY *laughs and* ELROY *smiles.*) But we do have to work once in a while. Like now. I have to do my messenger bit. Check you in the future. (*He begins to leave.*)

CANTOR: You be wishing you're back in the old country when you realize you're just cutting more sugar cane.

(*The elevator bell rings.* ELROY *opens the door.*)

SWIFTY: (*Offstage.*) Hey, hold the door! (SWIFTY *runs in dragging a handtruck loaded with more boxes.*)

JAY: Where you been?

ELROY: Long time no see.

SWIFTY: (*Agitatedly.*) That old guy had me stalled like we don't get hungry or something. Sat there pulling my own. Missed my whole munch hour.

ELROY: He'll let you eat now.

SWIFTY: He better. I'm hungry. (*He enters the elevator with his handtruck.*)

JAY: (*To* CANTOR.) Lotsa people hungry, man. (JAY *exits.*)

CANTOR: (*Shouting.*) Cane cutter!

(ELROY *and* SWIFTY *exit up the shaft.* CANTOR *is left alone. He takes off his sunglasses and puts them in a pocket. His legs buckle and he falls into an open sack of garbage, sprawling into a human heap. He makes an attempt to get up, but collapses, falling backwards into one of the garbage cans. Propped up, with his back against the can, he loses consciousness.* ELROY *comes out of the elevator with* SWIFTY *following close at his heels.* SWIFTY *angrily rolls a handtruck with still more boxes piled onto it. Not seeing* CANTOR, *he kicks a garbage can as he passes.* SWIFTY *exits. The noise wakes* CANTOR.)

ELROY: There he is, sitting on his throne. With all his subjects gathered 'round.

CANTOR: (*He speaks dreamily as if he is not there.*) The way she wrinkles her nose up when she laughs. Like a tiny bunny. And she wiggles that little cottontail. I pay no mind of picking that cotton. (*He laughs.*)

ELROY: You're sitting in garbage, you got to spit it out, too?

CANTOR: (*Softly.*) She got that little birthmark on her cottontail and no one know but me. And that dimple in her chin. Those things make her special. Like God Almighty put divine markings on her. Private and public places so everybody knows she the special one.

ELROY: You're making a car wreck look good.

CANTOR: We been drinking with friends. She was in her car ready to pull out of the parking lot. Me hanging on the door. Looking her dimple right in the eye. I say, "Don't want to go back to my apartment all by myself. For a small place, it seems so big and empty. Just like to talk to someone nice." She opens the door. We get to her house, we talk and she says she got to go to bed. Say I can stay over, since I so far from home. I say, "Where?" She goes into the bedroom. She say, "Come here." I go in. She's sitting down on the bed and patting her hand beside her on the sheet. She wrinkle her nose. We just lay aside each other all night long. Like spoons, but didn't touch once.

ELROY: You're a diagram for a disaster zone.

CANTOR: Next night we make love. Soft and slow. Touch her birthmark, and she giggle.

ELROY: I got to get you out of here before someone comes.

CANTOR: Most tender, soft girl I ever see. Ever will. (*Sacredly.*) Laverne.

ELROY: You're talking crazy about your woman! Let me help you up. Maybe you can walk it off. You be fired. (ELROY *pulls* CANTOR *to his feet. Suddenly,* CANTOR *pushes* ELROY *violently, knocking him backward. He hits hard against the wall.*)

CANTOR: I'll kill her! I'll kill her! She gonna get a beating like she never knowed! Do me like that. She gonna eat teeth! Her throat gonna be one blood smile! I'll shoot a third eye right in the middle of her forehead! See what she can do and what she can't do! (ELROY *remains calm.* CANTOR *sinks back. He becomes confused, trying to piece words together to make sentences and sentences together to make thoughts.*) She the most beau . . . I give her everything I know how . . . I am something . . . Bring home the pay every week. Brand new washing machine . . . Take care of business at night . . . What more she—

ELROY: You took a detour off the main track.

CANTOR: (*Bitterly.*) I'll never forgive her. Never. She come crawling on all fours, I don't even spit on that dog. Don't even let her lick my feet. I hate the sight of her ugly face. She looking worse every day. Like a bulldog bitch in heat. (*His face lights up with pride.*) I showed her. I walked right into the apartment. Her bags were packed. Suitcase aside the bed. "You say I don't make enough money?" I scream at her. I slam a few hundred fresh green ones on the bed. Some bills still floating in the air. I look that bunny smack in the eyes and say, "Eat this salad if you're so hungry." (*His eyes fill with tears.*) She say I'm nothing. That I'll never amount to nothing. She say I was so proud before 'cause I had everything ahead of me. Now I been nowhere, and going nowhere. That I'm not a man. Just a peacock with no feathers. (*Angrily.*) She grabs her bags and leaves me. (*He takes a drink from his pint.* ELROY *gently takes the bottle away from him.*) She was so pure. (*His face turns ugly.*) Now I get slut love. I be tired when I come home, woman. Just a whore when she make love. (*He begins to cry.*) Please forgive me for last night. I was just trying to do what you said. Just trying to show you. I can get money. I can treat you better. I wanted to please you. To keep you. To hold you to me. I can't even breathe without you. Like all the air is knocked out. El-man, every capillary of my heart is in pain. Something so far inside me. I don't know what it's called. But it's busted. I am nothing. Nothing without her.

ELROY: (*Gently.*) Best be going. I'll tell your boss that you're sick and had to go home.

CANTOR: Laverne dead. (*Pause.*) Dead to me. She don't exist. Never been born. Never lived. Never loved.

ELROY: She lives. Laverne's just gone.

CANTOR: 'Verne who? Don't know no Laverne. I be myself. Alone. Naked. Something. Me.

ELROY: I'll get you to the subway. (*He helps* CANTOR *to his feet.* CANTOR *fishes in his pocket for his bottle.*)

CANTOR: Where's my friend?

ELROY: Don't need that kind of friend.

CANTOR: Straight. (*Pause.*) Thanks for being here, Elroy. (CANTOR *leans on* ELROY *for support as they walk toward the subway.* SWIFTY *enters in a half-run. The boxes on his handtruck have grown in number. He takes sloppy sips from a can of beer.* CANTOR *jumps away from* ELROY, *wipes his face with a sleeve, and throws on his sunglasses. He stands tall and controlled, playing the macho-cool role with confidence.*)

SWIFTY: I'm wasting away on this job. My stomach's shrunk and my ribs are sticking out!

CANTOR: (*Very cool, with a smirk.*) If you can't hold your end up on the job, how you going to hold her end up in the sack?

SWIFTY: (*Sharply.*) I'm in no mood, smooth. Don't mess. (*The elevator bell rings.*)

ELROY: Stay here, Cant. I'll be right back. (*To* SWIFTY.) Going up?

SWIFTY: Got to catch my breath.

(ELROY *goes up the shaft as* SWIFTY *takes a long pull of beer.*)

CANTOR: You ain't making the scene with the building limousine, 'cause your taking an inhale of "catch-my-breath" ale.

SWIFTY: (*Irritably.*) Don't you got nothing better to do than spreading noise pollution? Like work?

CANTOR: (*Arrogantly.*) Woa! Don't ride the tide of your emotions, my man. Balance on the crest of the wave 'til you slide into the state of mind sands of ultra-cool, togetherness, and supra-sexual magnetism. (*Gesturing to himself.*) Like your main man here. I never let life be strife. Heed the advice.

(ELROY *opens the elevator door.*)

ELROY: False alarm.

SWIFTY: Get me upstairs. I'm fainting of hunger and jive.

ELROY: (*To* CANTOR.) Be cool and stay here. Sustain yourself.

(ELROY *takes* SWIFTY *upstairs.* CANTOR *tips backwards. He catches himself with his feet, one after the other, so he walks jerkily in reverse until a garbage can catches him at the knees, folding him into a sitting position. His head leans against the wall behind him and his jaw juts upward as he loses consciousness.* JAY *enters from the street. He goes to the elevator and rings the bell. At this alarm,* CANTOR *springs up wide-eyed and finds himself standing on top of the garbage can. He is animated and continues in reality what he was dreaming. He revels, as if seized with religious fervor.*)

CANTOR: I'm busting out of here! I'm ripping myself out of the guts of this building! This womb that's been carrying me these last nine years! I'm Caesarean myself away from here! This here shaft is a tight bitch, small frame and narrow bones, but I'll slice my way out! Break through this muscle fiber and tear through the navel of this place! Cut through the fat skin of this hole of my own will! Deliver myself from this shaft of my own power!

JAY: (*Amazed.*) What's the matter with you, man? Have you taken up Jesus?

CANTOR: (*He looks at* JAY, *then the garbage can, dazedly.*) How'd I get up here?

JAY: You're flying. How else?

CANTOR: (*He shakes himself out of his trance.*) I'm leaving her, Jay. It's definite. I'm leaving her.

JAY: Her?

CANTOR: Her.

JAY: Her who?

CANTOR: You know her who.

JAY: How I know her who?

CANTOR: Laverne. Who else? I'm blasting out on my own. She won't catch me if she was travelling the speed of light! I'm leaving her. Now! Soon. I feel it. Anytime. Me. Going. Busting out!

JAY: You leaving your woman?

CANTOR: The woman and this job.

JAY: Sorry to hear that.

(*Pause.*)

CANTOR: She invades who I am.

JAY: Isn't that what a woman supposed to do? Isn't that what a man and a woman are about? To invade every part of each other?

CANTOR: Y'see, Trinidad, Laverne wants to keep me on one level. This level. She ain't hungry enough. She's full and sleepy like after a good meal, when I ain't even stopped the growl in my stomach. She just wants that check on Friday. I come home, watch T.V., and take care of business at night. But I want more. Better. It's like she's getting off at the third floor and I want to go to the top floor! I want to go even higher! Higher than the top! The floor above the top floor! The floor above the roof. Bust through the roof and let me off at the clouds!

JAY: She's going to hurt.

CANTOR: Guilt is a useless emotion. (*Stumbling, struggling and getting frustrated at himself.*) She said to me that she has a responsibility to herself—I mean—I said to her that I have a responsibility to do what's best for me. And if my man—I mean—my woman—don't want what's best for me, then she's got to—I got to go. That's what she said—I said to her.

Scene Two

JAY: You're a mess.

CANTOR: I'm just excited that I'm single again.

JAY: It's none of my business, man, but don't you think you can give her another chance?

CANTOR: I've sold her enough raffle tickets, and she lost.

JAY: But maybe you can work it out.

CANTOR: I'm cement.

JAY: A man is meant to be with a woman. To hold on to each other through the bad times so it's better when the good times come around.

CANTOR: Quit butting in.

JAY: She's your root.

CANTOR: I said stick to yourself.

JAY: You've been through so much together.

CANTOR: (*Angrily.*) I don't want to hear it.

JAY: You shouldn't make any decision drunk the way you are.

CANTOR: Get your nose out of my life!

JAY: Sober up and think it over.

CANTOR: You want a fat lip, fat lips?

JAY: Think how you'll miss her.

CANTOR: Shut up.

JAY: When you roll over in the morning, your arm is feeling for her and she's not there.

CANTOR: Do you know what shut up means?

JAY: It'll be hard to carry on.

CANTOR: Said clam, Sam!

JAY: Hard to get another woman who's gone through as much as you and Laverne have.

CANTOR: Shut up.

JAY: She's gone. (CANTOR *swings at* JAY, *who easily avoids the punch.* JAY *plants a fisted arm like a ramrod into* CANTOR'S *stomach.* CANTOR *crumbles to the ground with no argument. He is unconscious again.*) Red-blooded Americans. (JAY *shakes* CANTOR *awake and helps him to his feet.*)

CANTOR: Who won?

JAY: No one had to peel me off the sidewalk.

CANTOR: I would of hit you if I wasn't so busy hitting the bottle.

JAY: All in good fun.

CANTOR: (*To himself.*) I am somebody. (*He laughs a low rumble.*) What a joke, Jesse. I need a drink.

JAY: You sure, man?

CANTOR: Jay, that's the only thing I am sure of.

SCENE TWO

(CANTOR *lifts his frame tall and cockily. He struts down the street whistling a light tune. When he is just out of sight,* ELROY *and* SWIFTY *come off the elevator. Strapped on* SWIFTY'S *handtruck are even more boxes. He flushes with anger and frustration.*)

ELROY: Got to cool out now. It ain't but a job. They don't know nothing up there anyhow. Don't know their head from their butt. (SWIFTY *exits in the same direction as* CANTOR.) Where the heck is Cantor?

JAY: I got to talk to you for a moment, man.

ELROY: Sorry, Jay, but I ain't got the time. Got to find Cant. (*He looks up and down the street.*) I should of handcuffed him to the lamppost. I know that boy's in trouble. Hope he ain't sniffing around that liquor store again.

JAY: He said he'd be right back. Don't worry. I got to ask you a favor, El-man.

ELROY: Well, so long as Cantor be coming. Shoot Jay, you got me bagged. Fire away.

JAY: A friend was going to drive me to Kennedy Airport tonight but his car broke down.

ELROY: What you playing with planes for?

JAY: My wife's on one from Trinidad.

ELROY: Say, hey! No fooling! A wife! Well, damn, man! Why you been so cloak and dagger?

JAY: (*Smiling.*) And a beautiful girl.

ELROY: Say you Satan! Congratulations! Espionage and all.

JAY: I didn't mean to cover it up.

ELROY: You were doing a heck of a Watergate.

JAY: It just never came up.

ELROY: Especially with your girlfriends. I'm sure. (*They laugh.*)

JAY: Could you drive me to pick them up after work?

ELROY: Course I can. Be happy to, Jay. But well, well. That's news. Something all right. A wife and kid. And no one knowed. Why they coming of a sudden?

JAY: I have the money now. I can support them. Live good. It's been so long since I've seen them. It's hard to get out of Trinidad. Expensive. I'm lucky to be here myself. If I ever went back, I'm not sure I could get out again.

ELROY: Well that's great they're coming, Jay. Really is.

JAY: My whole purpose has been to get them here. They've been staying at her parents' house. (*His eyes sparkle.*) I want you to see my daughter. An island princess, truly.

ELROY: How old?

JAY: Was three, so now four.

ELROY: That so.

JAY: Yeah. She's the pride of my life, man. She's so alive. So fresh.

ELROY: Kids are something all right. My rat pack is a terror.

JAY: At two years old, she was in the sea with a blown-up inner tube. Riding the waves like a cork.

ELROY: My one boy, Bobby, he can slam his head flat onto a radiator and he'll complain about his knee. (JAY *laughs.*) One time Bobby was walking with a hot dog and some french fries. He trips over his own feet 'cause he's so busy stuffing his face. The wiener goes one way and the fries the other. He falls down and the palm of his hand slams onto a busted bottle lying on the sidewalk. He gets up with blood streaming down his arm crying his eyes out. My wife is yelling, "Don't look at the cut!" Bobby, with tears all over his face, says, "What cut? I only got one bite of that dog and two greasy fries." (*They both laugh.*)

JAY: No kidding?

ELROY: Yeah. That kid is something. When I walk through that door at night the whole gang of them swing on me like a jungle gym.

JAY: My girl is very intelligent. Before I left, she could count to ten and write her name. My wife teaches her good.

ELROY: (*Proudly.*) My other boy, he was flying like a bullet on a bike out of the alley, pops a wheely over the curb, springs from his banana seat, over his angel bars, and the corner of a building takes a chunk out of his skull. The nurse shaves a circle on the top of his head and when he was taking some stitches that boy just bit his lip. His eyes teared up, but he don't make a whimper, not a sound. He was a good boy. (*Pause.*) Going to be a good man when he grow. Gave him some ice cream.

JAY: My wife fixes my daughter's hair in these little rolls. Look very nice, man.

ELROY: Yeah, my wife does up my two girls for Sunday school in pink ribbons. They look kind of funny, but they're cute.

(*Pause.*)

JAY: Y'know El-man, when this job gets me down, and I can't take it anymore, I make my mind far away and think of my little girl. I remember when she was born. I was there with the birthing. So easy, the delivery. Only seven pushes my wife had. And the baby came with no crying. The doctor put her on my wife's stomach and the baby smiled at me. Gums. No crying. Smiling right at me. (*Pause.*) She's going to be a true American. Raised American. I am so proud of that. Trinidad will always be a part of me. A claim on my soul but not hers. The island will be in her blood and that blood passed on, but she'll be of this northern island. Manhattan. And that's good.

ELROY: I'm happy for you.

JAY: Work'll be so much easier to take. My baby'll be my reward when I go home. (*His eyes become distant.*) My child is so lovely, man. Her face is precisely symmetric. Big, round cheeks sculpted out of black clay. Her nose perfectly chiseled. Her ears flawless. And her eyes are like the sea at night. Beautifully black against white sand. Big and deep. Life breathes beyond the surface. Her eyes sparkle like moonbeams on waves. My baby's eyes. Moon on the Caribbean.

ELROY: She must be beautiful.

JAY: The most beautiful in Trinidad. In the Caribbean.

ELROY: In the world.

SCENE TWO

(JAY *looks at him questioningly, and then laughs.* ELROY *smiles.*)

JAY: (*Jokingly.*) In the universe, man! (*Pause.*) But you'll drive me to the airport?

ELROY: You bet.

JAY: The plane checks in at seven, so maybe we can catch a drink before we go.

ELROY: Sounds good. Be meeting your family. Privileged.

JAY: Thanks, man. They're coming in legal, too. Not like me. (JAY *laughs.*) That's worry off my mind. Can you get this illegal alien up to the third floor?

ELROY: It's my bread and butter.

(*They cross to the elevator.*)

JAY: Cantor and me got into a tuft.

ELROY: Heck no.

JAY: Say yes. And I don't even know what it was about. He swung first, but I duked him soft. Spread him on the floor like caviar on pumpernickel.

(*They enter the elevator.*)

ELROY: Got to snoop his trail.

JAY: He's at the liquor store.

ELROY: I knew it. I'll go get him.

(*They go up the shaft.* SWIFTY *enters from the street. His handtruck is empty. He parks the truck to the side. He stands in contained silence.*

His tee shirt is drenched with sweat. He suddenly paces with jittery movement. His arm lashes out sporadically. His pacing becomes quicker and more jerky. He abruptly stops. Silence. His face flushes. He bolts to a garbage can, kicks it, then throws the can at the handtruck. ELROY *emerges from the elevator.* SWIFTY *kicks the handtruck and throws himself against a wall.* ELROY *runs to* SWIFTY *and wraps his arms around him from behind in a bear hug.* SWIFTY *does not fight* ELROY, *and allows himself to be held.* SWIFTY *almost hyperventilates. His breathing regulates.* ELROY *releases him.* ELROY *takes* CANTOR'S *pint of Wild Turkey out of his pocket and offers the whiskey to* SWIFTY. SWIFTY *takes a powerful slug. He gives the bottle back to* ELROY. ELROY *wipes the mouth of the bottle with his shirt and takes a drink.* SWIFTY *pulls out a joint from his sock, lights it, takes a drag, and holds the cigarette out to* ELROY, *who shakes his head in polite refusal.* ELROY *offers him the pint again.* SWIFTY *takes it. He raises the marijuana in one hand and the whiskey in the other.*)

SWIFTY: Dope to control the dopes! (SWIFTY *takes a hit of the joint, another slug of booze, swallows, then exhales the smoke in a tremendous sigh of control.*)

ELROY: What happened?

SWIFTY: Old Boneface upstairs told me to go down to Rublin's again, for the hundreth time today. To the same place. A couple of trips ago, he forgets to write on the order sheet to pick up a sample of the Suzie Throw-Up Doll, or whatever the name of the doll is. The doll's supposed to do everything. This I got to see. I know he wants the doll but he forgets to put it on the list. So I tell Rublin to lay some Suzie Suck dolls on me or whatever the name is, right? Nothing. Jerk looks at me like I'm talking Lebanese. I write it on the list. He turns the paper sideways like I'm writing Chink. My boss wants the Suzie sample doll. The guy won't give it to me. (*Getting angry again.*) Like I can't bring something back

Scene Two

on my own. Like it's nothing out of this guy's nose to give me one ratty bottle-in-her-mouth, Suzie-wets, goddamn sample doll! Like I don't got a brain! I can't think! I need a note to pick up any kind of ding-dong, do-do, bow-wow toy! Some kind of tinker-type, piss piece of trinket! So I come back. Tell el bosso. He yells at me why didn't I remind him when I was making out the order sheet in the first place. He sends me right out the door again. But first, he writes the addres on the note. Like I don't remember where this latrine I go to a million times a day is. To that little kike hades they call a warehouse. This armpit of a Jewish palace. Stinks like bad pork. Give me some head cheese, suck some kosher pickle, and eat some matzoh balls, man!

ELROY: Calm. (*Pause.*) Breathe.

(SWIFTY *breathes. He takes another drink and a hit of the joint.*)

SWIFTY: Like I'm a retard. Some kind of slave. One of these days when I hear my boss on the phone and he says, "I'll send my boy over with a note. Make sure he takes the right package; he's a little spaced." And he laughs; comes up to me with that note. Tells me what to do. I say, "No," and smash him right in the mouth so hard I shove three thousand dollars worth of caps right down his pipe!

ELROY: And you'll get three thousand years of jail time.

SWIFTY: Just once.

ELROY: One too many.

(*Silence.*)

SWIFTY: What do I got to lose? It's like I'm already in the pen. Like I'm handcuffed and busted. They're frisking me and I don't got nothing. I'm clean. Don't own a damn thing. What's my crime? Somebody's got to do the job and I do it. That's what they want. I answer an ad in the paper, they hire me, then they treat me like a criminal. Like I did something wrong. All I do is do what they say. (*He seethes with frustration.*) That's what they want. So why do they think I'm an idiot? Doing what they say? Makes me want to do something bad. To them. To anyone. I got eyes I see. Ears I hear. Brain I think. They treat me like a lump of human muscle. Like I don't know what's going on. Like I can't sense their attitude. Like I won't flinch when they bite me. (*The elevator bell rings.*) I get along with people. But these guys make me feel like I don't belong. I don't understand. I don't know why they treat me like that. (*The bell rings again.*) I don't want to go to school. I don't want to wear a suit. I don't want to be the boss. I don't want to make tons of money. I JUST WANT TO MAKE A LIVING FOR MY WIFE AND KIDS. WHAT IN HELL'S NAME IS WRONG WITH THAT? (*The bell rings again.*) What is so stupid about that? Why do they think that's dumb? Sometimes I just want to kick this job in the balls!

(*The bell rings.*)

ELROY: Easy.

SWIFTY: This is my job! This is how my kids eat! This is how my kids get an education! This is how my wife can buy a dress and get her hair done! (*The bell is rung several times impatiently in quick bursts.* SWIFTY *hits his head in frustration. His eyes search.*) I don't get it. (*Silence.*) The thing is, talk about stupid. Boneface upstairs can't even say Rublin's name. One Jew to another. He knows this guy like lox on a bagel with cream cheese. Been robbing the Hebe blind for forty years, right? Everytime he tries to say his name, he twists up his face, pulls back his lips, shows those green horse teeth

SCENE TWO 37

and breathes this puking exhaust out of his tail-pipe of a mouth with, "Luble". (ELROY *laughs a low rumble.*) How does he get "Luble" out of "Rublin"? (ELROY'S *laugh expands.* SWIFTY *imitates his boss with an exaggerated accent and a grotesque version of a face.*) "Lun to Luble's and letuln wit' a hald buttelt loll."

(ELROY *howls and* SWIFTY *laughs with him.* SWIFTY'S *laugh is so hysterical that his eyes tear up with the release. Eventually both men calm down. They catch their breath as* SWIFTY *wipes his eyes with his shirt. They both sigh, giggling here and there.*)

ELROY: Y'know what I do when I feel like I am the elevator? Like the elevator's running me instead of me running the elevator? When I feel I'm just a piece of this building? No different than a box of steel or a line of cable? (*Pause.*) I think of sex. (*Pause.*) That's what I do. (*Pause.*) All day. (*Pause.*) That's my drug. (*Pause.*) That's what dulls me to this job. To what I see happening. To life. (*Pause.*) Everybody has something. Some guys drink. Some folk smoke hash. Blow snow. People pop pills. (*Pause.*) I think of sex. (*Pause.*) And do sex. As often as possible. (*Pause.*) Y'see, some dudes get off more when they're bragging how good they are, than when they're actually doing it. They walk with a stick down their leg talking about ladies, but when they're up to bat for real, they can't swing it. (*Pause.*) See, talk wastes your energy. You talk it, you get it out of your system. I contain it. I prize it. Keep it secret in me. I hide it from everbody so I don't lose it. Or it don't get stole. And when it's a tight, boiling, built-up, ready-to-bust fortune, I throw the combination, open the safe, and unlock all that magic stuff coming from way down deep inside me and release it into a woman. (*Pause.*) That's how I beat life. (*Pause.*) I like all women. Ain't never seen a woman that I wasn't attracted to. Now there is better than others, but I don't think it's in God to make an ugly woman. To me it don't matter race, age, shape, nor attitude. Most men I know take what they can get. And I like to take them all. (*Pause.*) What woman got is my survival.

(*Silence.*)

SWIFTY: I get crazy looking at girls on the street. I goof with them. But when I go home and see my wife, I'm always shocked at how beautiful she is. I never remember her looking so great. Like I lost my memory. What do I want with women on the street? She's the liquor that makes me forget the day. I get drunk out of my mind over her. And in bed I'm a regular alcoholic. You ain't never met her, have you? My wife.

ELROY: Never had the privilege.

SWIFTY: She's gorgeous. Big bust. Hips. Made for love. When I walk in that door, I belong. It's not that I'm king of the castle or something, it's just that I'm whole. Part of a whole that's bigger than me. I ain't boxed in or busted up. I belong. We do each other good. I look up to her. She looks up to me. I pull her up and push her above me. Then she pulls me up level and pushes me above her. And I pull her up and she pulls me up. And we go higher and higher. We just keep holding onto and climbing into each other and spiraling above and beyond what we thought could be.

ELROY: I know that feeling of climbing. My elevator. You want to break through the ceiling. That urge to get to the floor above the roof.

(*Pause.*)

SWIFTY: I love her. (*Silence.*) Better get going. I got one more load to pick up. (*He gets his handtruck and starts down the street. He stops and turns to face* ELROY.) El. Thanks, man. Check it.

Scene Two

ELROY: Checked.

(SWIFTY *exits.* JAY *enters from the stairwell area.*)

JAY: I was ringing like a church bell at noon.

ELROY: Sorry, man. (*The bell rings.*) Damn! I'm a fool to this bell! (ELROY *goes up in the elevator. Suddenly, there is offstage commotion.*)

JAY: (*Yelling down the street.*) Hey, what's going on? (*Running offstage.*) What's happening!

(*Scuffling and the explosive voices of* SWIFTY, CANTOR, JAY *and two other men are heard offstage. The voices are hysterical but for the most part unintelligible. The stage is empty for this brief time. Clear phrases shoot out intermittently.*)

CANTOR: I did it for her—

VOICE: In stable condition—

CANTOR: She made me do it—

SWIFTY: Shut up, you fool—

VOICE: Can't believe he came to work—

SWIFTY and JAY: (*Simultaneously.*) Shut up!

VOICE: Immigrant—

(ELROY *comes out of the elevator, almost colliding with* SWIFTY, *who sprints onstage.* SWIFTY *throws his handtruck to the side and wipes his bleeding forehead with a handkerchief.* SWIFTY *verbally explodes with the speed of lightning. When* ELROY *speaks, they overlap lines.*)

ELROY: What happened to you?

SWIFTY: I'm slipping down the street when I see two guys got Cantor up against a wall. One guy makes Cantor's arm a pretzel. I'm booking across the street. This goon's got Cant's gut kissing the sidewalk. I'm not even touching the ground. I'm shooting like a bullet with teeth. I clip one guy in the left temple—bip—kick him in the breadbasket—bop—the other dude dukes me a clean shot in the shoulder—zap—Cantor still eating cement. He's mumbling, "Don't bust the fuzz." I stop punching stone cold. I drop my arms in a daze. That's when the dick takes a tally of my facial features with his fist—boom—pokes a dent in my forehead. Wearing a spiked ring. That's when I tackle him. That's when I'm kicking that joke in the ribs and popping off his kneecap. Police or no. He hit me when the play was over. The whistle been blown.

ELROY: That a boy.

SWIFTY: The other pig's mashing my ear into a cauliflower. All of a sudden, I look up and see Jay-man falling on us from the sky. Out of thin air.

ELROY: The black plague.

SWIFTY: Jay's fist is red coming out of the cop's mouth. This hard-nose gives a dog yelp. Jay's operating on his chest.

ELROY: Little heart surgery.

SWIFTY: A chip of steel clips my chin. I'm nose to nose with six cylinders. Something makes a big click. The games over. Our hands are up with barrels of lead everywhere. Dicks tell us to hold up the wall. Three of us against brick with our legs being kicked apart. Cantor's so drunk, the wall's holding him up. He mumbles that us two got nothing to do with nothing. We're just friends and don't know that they're the law. My face, his, hot and wet. Blood running like a south stream. They say they was busting Cantor for armed robbery and assault with a deadly weapon. You believe that? Knocked over a gas station last night. An alarm spooked him. He spun around and winged a guy.

ELROY: Damn.

SWIFTY: But then he didn't even run. He walks down the middle of the street right to his apartment. Goes through the front door and flips on the lights. One of the gas station attendants followed him and saw him yelling at Laverne through the window. He sees Cant throw the money on the bed. There's a crash and then the guy eyeballs a revolver hitting the pavement with pieces of glass chasing it. Cant says she made him do it. Jay and I say shut up, you idiot. Cops say they didn't think he was dumb enough to go to work. They been staking his place. And there he is whistling down the street. Then the pig that Jay had just skinned gives Jay a wild look. The cop looked like he had a golf ball in his mouth. Jay had really done a number on him. The cop wants him bad. Blood in his eyes. Says, "What's your name, boy? You got identification?" Jay says his name and tells him where he lives. But he's talking with his accent, y'know?

ELROY: Oh, man.

SWIFTY: "You an immigrant? Where's your green card?" and like that. Sweat bubbling on Jay's brow. He makes a break. There's a tube of steel sticking in the back of my neck. I don't move. The cop nabs Jay and feeds him a brick wall for dinner. His face all scraped. They cuff both Jay and Cant. Tell me to beat it unless I want to try on some steel jewelry, too. Cantor mumbling about Laverne. How beautiful she is. What a pig she is. How she made him do it. Jay cracking jokes. They both trying to laugh. A wagon pulls up and the dicks throw them in. Then I run into you, man. (*Silence.* SWIFTY *folds his arms trying to contain himself. He breathes hard. Neither of them know what to say. The two men stare at each other. They look down the street. They look at the elevator. They are full of incomplete actions and emotions, not knowing what course of action to take, if any.*) GODDAMN IT! (*He paces, still nursing his wounds.*) GODDAMN IT! I wanted to kill those cops!

ELROY: But Cantor did wrong. Shot a man.

SWIFTY: He didn't even fight them. We were the ones.

ELROY: Like he wanted to get caught.

SWIFTY: And Jay, goddamn it! If he knew they were cops, he wouldn't have stepped in.

ELROY: Don't know about that. When a friend's in trouble—

SWIFTY: Why'd Cantor come to work?

ELROY: Like he wanted to get caught. I knew he had done something.

SWIFTY: They're going to break up Jay in the back of that wagon. That cop was hurting.

ELROY: Laverne left him.

SWIFTY: No woman can make you shoot a man.

ELROY: Cantor always said he had a gun at the apartment for protection.

Scene Two

SWIFTY: They'll send Jay back to Trinidad.

ELROY: Everybody goes crazy every once while. I'm always glad I don't got a gun in the house when I go nuts.

SWIFTY: Cantor going to be behind monkey bars. He was admitting to it. We were yelling shut up!

ELROY: Laverne cut his cables. He fell to the basement and come crawling to this elevator shaft. Back to the womb where it's safe. Found him here this morning.

SWIFTY: Like he was proving something to Laverne with that gas station number.

ELROY: She busted him.

(*Silence.*)

SWIFTY: I don't know.

ELROY: I don't either.

SWIFTY: (*Quietly.*) Goddamn it.

(*Silence.*)

ELROY: I had one of my elevator dreams last night. What they call a recurring dream. It's always the same. Always starts with machinery. Giant cables and iron doors. Brass and bolts. The machine pumps. I don't have to go in, but I always do. I need the elevator to go to a certain floor. I got to go up. Get higher. I go in, press the button, and the box starts to climb. There's nothing I can do. It's already too late. There I am, trapped in steel like I'm caught in the machinery. I can't get out. There's no ceiling on the box so I can see all the trappings. The cables and the light at the top of the shaft. That's the floor I want to get to. To that light. To the floor above the roof. I know everything'll be fine once I get to that floor. And then it happens. The box slants. I try to keep my footing. It slants the other way. It throws me. My balance is a wreck. I can see down the shaft. Way down to the basement. Total dark. Black. Then bam! The cable snaps. The upward mobility stops and I start a slow fall. The floors go past me. Like a backward count to death—27—26—25. Faster and faster 'til they're flying by!—18—17—16—15. I'm pressing the buttons of the floors I haven't hit yet. Maybe they'll catch and lock. They don't. I'm slamming buttons. I'm jumping up, trying to climb over the walls, maybe I can get a hold of something. A steady cable or hold onto one of the lower floors before I hit the basement. I can't get a grip. I'm part of this busted machine. I'm part of it. A piece of steel. I'm plunging to the basement and I can't do nothing! I see the first floor go flashing by. And bam! I'm sitting up in bed. I'm doing the silent scream act. Cold sweat bit. I try to catch my breath. Shake my head. Sigh. I know what happened. I got sucked in by my elevator dream again. Then I get up. Come to work. Climb into this shaft. And hope my nightmare don't become real. (*Pause.*) But y'know, Swifty, sometimes I think it already has. I ain't never fell down the shaft, but sometimes I think my nightmare has come true.

SWIFTY: Hey, El, you're the rock of Gibraltar. I can't see anyone else running this box.

ELROY: Oh, I got this shaft all by myself. This shaft is mine. Somebody try to take my pretty little box from me, I kill him. (*He pounds the elevator door and laughs.*) This purring sweetheart's mine! (*He rubs the elevator sensuously.*) And I'm a jealous man. (*He laughs.*)

SWIFTY: There you are!

ELROY: Yeah. We're lucky.

SWIFTY: Oh. I almost forgot. Jay said to me, "Tell Elroy that my blood is here."

ELROY: You got those toys you traded with Jay?

SWIFTY: Got them in the back.

ELROY: I know who he wanted to give them to. Can I have them?

SWIFTY: Sure. I got to walk this horse to the stable anyway. (SWIFTY *exits out the stairwell with his handtruck. He returns quickly wearing a turquoise jacket and a pair of sunglasses. He carries a bag filled with toys and Jay's box radio.*) Take Jay's box, too. I already got one. (*He hands* ELROY *the bag, radio, and wrap-around sunglasses.*) The shades are from Cantor. He never got to give his radio to Laverne.

ELROY: (*Putting on the sunglasses.*) She already tuned him out.

SWIFTY: I ain't picking up that last load. I quit this kick of a day. I ain't even going upstairs. Boneface can figure it out that I left. What you doing tonight?

ELROY: Thought I'd go to the airport and watch some planes come down the runway.

SWIFTY: What for?

ELROY: Tell you tomorrow. First I got to cancel a date I got downstairs. She's supposed to come through the alleyway.

SWIFTY: Say "Hi" to your wife for me.

ELROY: And you yours from me.

SWIFTY: Yeah. I'm just going to lay back and put a bottle of my wife to my lips. Lose consciousness and forget. (*He looks up at the sky.*) Looks like rain.

ELROY: Maybe it'll cool us down.

SWIFTY: I got to cool out or I'm going to explode. (*They look at each other for a long silence.*) See you tomorrow with the birds. We climb up another one.

ELROY: Catch you when it dawns on us.

(SWIFTY *turns up his collar and exits down the street.* ELROY *enters the elevator shaft and slams the door with finality.*)

BLACKOUT

[END OF PLAY]

www.ingramcontent.com/pod-product-compliance
Lightning Source LLC
Chambersburg PA
CBHW060221050426
42446CB00013B/3137